ROMAN
GODS, HEROES, AND MYTHOLOGY

BY PATRICE SHERMAN

CONTENT CONSULTANT
Carl A. P. Ruck
Professor of Classical Studies
Boston University

Core Library

Cover image: Minerva, the goddess of wisdom and
sometimes war, is often shown with a helmet.

An Imprint of Abdo Publishing
abdobooks.com

abdocorelibrary.com

Published by Abdo Publishing, a division of ABDO, PO Box 398166, Minneapolis, Minnesota 55439. Copyright © 2019 by Abdo Consulting Group, Inc. International copyrights reserved in all countries. No part of this book may be reproduced in any form without written permission from the publisher. Core Library™ is a trademark and logo of Abdo Publishing.

Printed in the United States of America, North Mankato, Minnesota
092018
012019

Cover Photo: Fine Art Images/Heritage Images/Hulton Fine Art Collection/Getty Images
Interior Photos: Fine Art Images/Heritage Images/Hulton Fine Art Collection/Getty Images, 1, 32; iStockphoto, 4–5, 11 (top), 36–37, 43; New York Public Library/Science Source, 7, 17, 19; Viroj Phetchkhum/Shutterstock Images, 11 (bottom); Art Media/Print Collector/Hulton Archive/Getty Images, 14–15; Fine Art Images Heritage Images/Newscom, 22–23, 28–29, 45; De Agostini Editorial/Getty Images, 25; Theodore Clutter/Science Source, 31; Kizel Cotiw–an/Shutterstock Images, 38; Christos Georghiou/Shutterstock Images, 41

Editor: Marie Pearson
Series Designer: Ryan Gale

Library of Congress Control Number: 2018949766

Publisher's Cataloging-in-Publication Data

Names: Sherman, Patrice, author.
Title: Roman gods, heroes, and mythology / by Patrice Sherman.
Description: Minneapolis, Minnesota : Abdo Publishing, 2019 | Series: Gods, heroes, and mythology | Includes online resources and index.
Identifiers: ISBN 9781532117862 (lib. bdg.) | ISBN 9781532170720 (ebook)
Subjects: LCSH: Roman mythology--Juvenile literature. | Roman gods--Juvenile literature. | Heroes--Juvenile literature.
Classification: DDC 292.13--dc23

CONTENTS

CHAPTER ONE

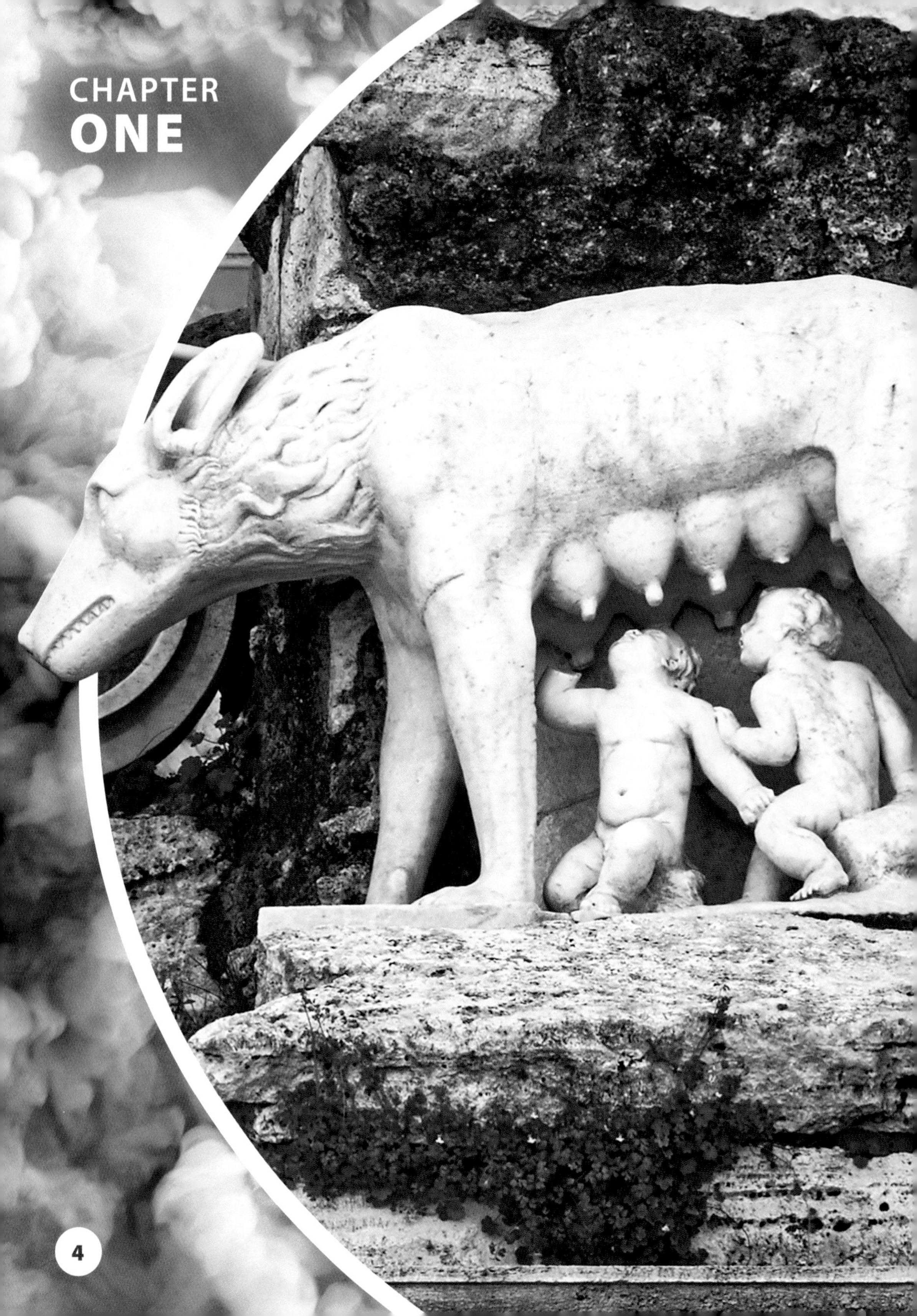

THE ORIGINS OF ROME

R omulus and Remus were alone in the world. They lay crying in a basket on the shores of the River Tiber, hungry and cold, with no one to protect them. Yet these abandoned twins were princes with royal blood. Their grandfather King Numitor had ruled the city of Alba Longa, in the region of Latium. But the king's brother, Amulius, had seized power. He forced Numitor into exile far from the city.

Amulius wanted to make sure that Numitor had no descendants to claim the throne. When the king's daughter, Rhea Silvia, gave birth to

A wolf cared for infants Romulus and Remus.

Romulus and Remus, Amulius had ordered a servant to drown the newborn infants in the river.

The servant, however, could not bring himself to murder two helpless babies. So he put them in a basket woven from reeds and sent them down the river. After traveling for several hours, the basket washed up on the shore near the Palatine Hill.

As the twin infants lay crying, a female wolf padded up to the basket and sniffed them. She licked them. Then she did something extraordinary. She picked the infants up in her jaws, one by one, and carried them back to her den. There, she nursed them along with her own wolf cubs. The boys grew strong on the wolf's milk. One day, a shepherd found them and took them back to his house. He and his wife raised them as their own sons. Romulus and Remus became shepherds like their adoptive father.

One day, they were grazing their flocks on a hillside. Several shepherds who worked for King Amulius

The shepherd who found and cared for Romulus and Remus was named Faustulus.

ordered them away, telling them that the hill belonged to the king. Romulus and Remus refused to leave. A fight broke out. The king's shepherds captured Remus and brought him back to the city.

Romulus gathered a band of friends. They went to rescue his brother. They freed Remus and killed King Amulius. Numitor returned from exile and became King of Alba Longa once more.

WOLF CHILDREN

Many cultures have stories about children raised by wolves. Like humans, wolves live together in close family groups and care for their young. Perhaps that's why some people believe they might adopt human babies, who are very small and helpless like wolf pups. Children raised by wolves have been the subject of several books. These children are sometimes called feral, which means wild or untamed.

Romulus, Remus, and their friends set off to start their own city. The twins argued over where the city should be located. Finally, they decided to have a contest. They each stood on a hill. The hill with the most birds would be the new city's location. Birds were believed to be good omens, or signs, from the gods.

Romulus went to Palatine Hill, and Remus to Aventine Hill. Romulus saw twice as many birds. He won.

Romulus began to build a wall around Palatine Hill to protect his new city. Remus became jealous. He made fun of his brother, leaping over the wall to show

how small and weak it was. The brothers fought, and Romulus killed Remus. Afterward, he felt sorry. He honored Remus with a great funeral. He went on to build his city, which he called Roma, or Rome.

THE ROMAN EMPIRE

The story of Romulus and Remus is a foundation myth. The tale explains how Rome came to be founded, who founded it, and why. The ancient Romans had many such stories to explain their history and their culture. These tales were a way of passing down cultural values from one generation to the next. Myths shaped their identity, reminding them what it meant to be Roman.

Myths are stories that involve supernatural beings and events. For the Romans, the supernatural was not distant and mysterious. It was part of everyday life. They felt close to their gods and goddesses. They believed gods took part in human affairs. Before taking any important action, Romans would seek the favor of their gods through prayers and offerings. The offerings

OVID: POET OF ROME

Ovid was one of Rome's greatest poets. He wrote about mythology, nature, and Roman history. His long poem *Metamorphoses* tells how gods transformed people into rocks, trees, animals, stars, and other natural objects. His six-book poem *Fasti* records the important events and holidays Romans celebrated during the year. Ovid's works have been translated into many languages. People still read them today.

might be flowers, fruits, coins, or animals. When making a decision, Romans consulted the gods through auguries, or oracles. An oracle was a priest or priestess who looked for omens that would show a person the correct path to follow.

Every Roman city and town had a least one public temple. People would gather at the temple to honor the gods or seek their advice. Romans also worshipped their gods at home. Roman homes had at least one small altar dedicated to a household spirit or to the spirit of a deceased person. Family members placed offerings such as fruit or flowers at these altars. They asked the

A ROMAN
TEMPLE

The Pantheon, one of Rome's temples, stands as an important example of Roman architecture. It was built in 126 CE. The interior, where people worshipped, is the rotunda. The wall around the rotunda is the drum. The rotunda is topped by the dome. The hole in the dome is the oculus. The oculus was designed to let in light. Why do you think these features were important?

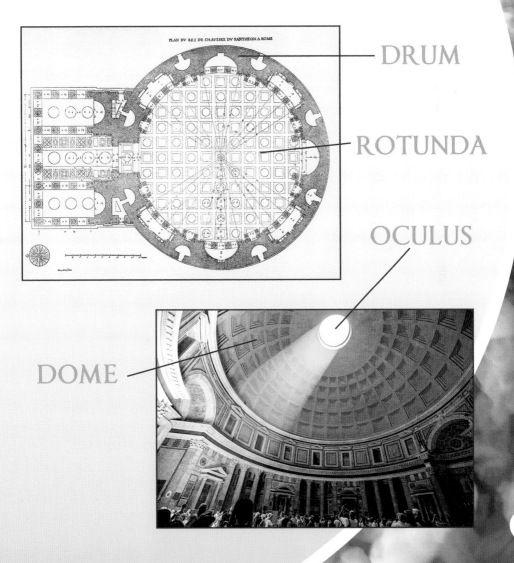

DRUM

ROTUNDA

OCULUS

DOME

spirit to protect the home and bring everyone in it health and good fortune.

For more than 400 years, Romans ruled over an empire that stretched from England to Turkey. The city of Rome was at its center. Romans were proud of their empire. They built roads and bridges to unite their territories. They designed aqueducts to deliver fresh water to cities and towns. Romans believed the gods favored them over their enemies. They did not expect the people they conquered to worship their gods. But Romans did expect these people to respect Roman laws. The laws kept peace throughout the empire. The Romans' rule ended when Rome fell to its enemies in 410 CE. But Rome's culture had a lasting influence on Western history. Roman art, architecture, engineering, and literature are still studied and admired today.

STRAIGHT TO THE
SOURCE

In his book *Fasti*, the Roman poet Ovid tells how Romulus and Remus decided who would rule their city (The word *swains* means "young men," and refers to their friends. *Hied* means "hurried."):

> *The twins agreed to draw the swains together and found a city; the doubt was which of the two should found it. Romulus said, "There needs no contest. Great faith is put in birds; let's try the birds." The proposal was accepted. One of the two betook him to the rocks of the wooded Palatine; the other hied at morn to the top of the Aventine. Remus saw six birds; Romulus saw twice six, one after the other: they stood by their compact, and Romulus was accorded the government of the city.*

> Source: "Ovid, Fasti, Book 4." Trans. James G. Frazer. *Theoi Greek Mythology*. Classical Texts Library, 2017. Web. Lines 809–813. Accessed June 1, 2018.

Consider Your Audience

Read the passage carefully. Then, try rewriting this story as a short skit to be performed for your classmates or friends. How do you think the twins would speak? How would you show the action of climbing hills and counting birds?

CHAPTER TWO

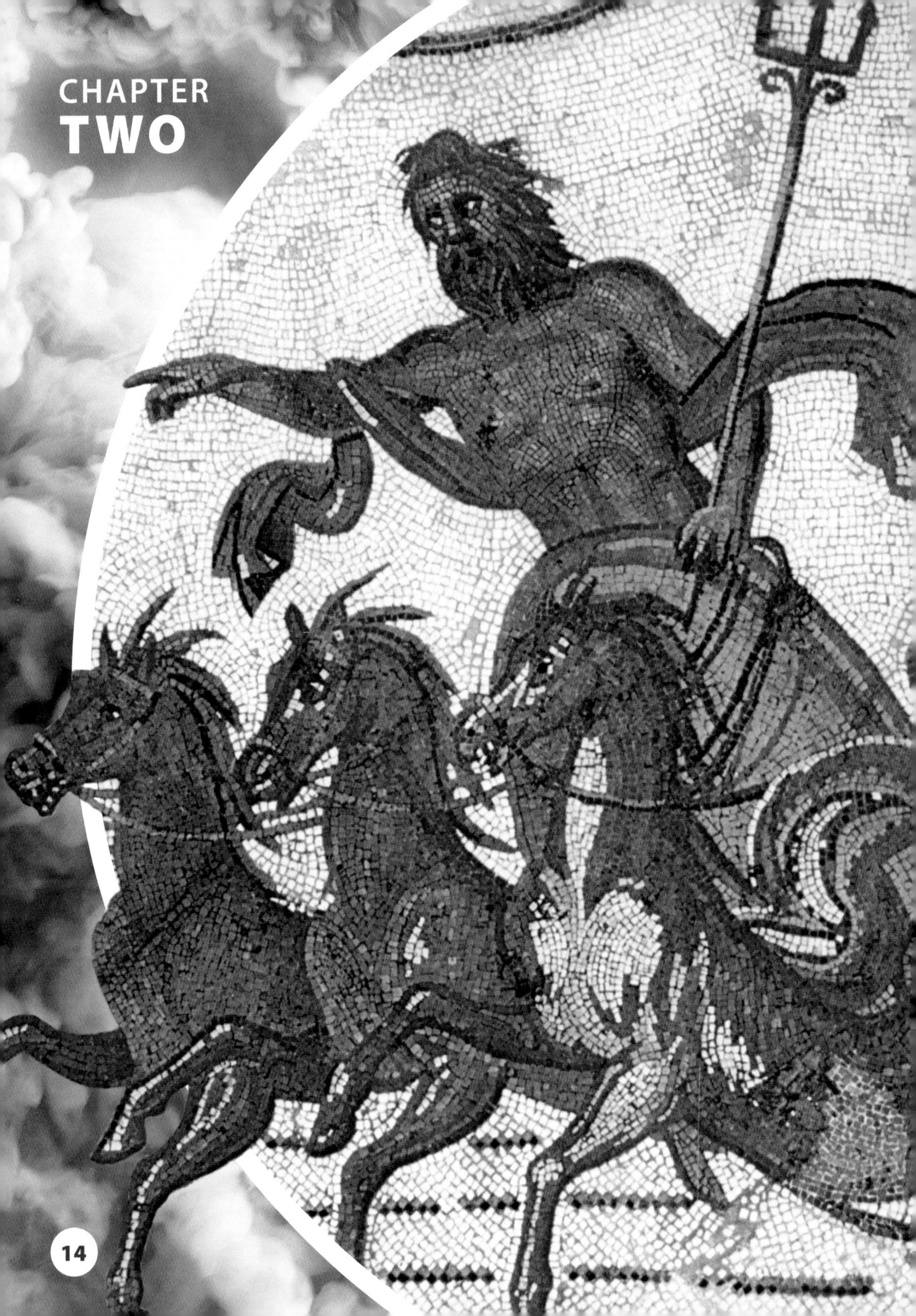

GODS AND GODDESSES

Romans were polytheists—they had many gods and goddesses. Every deity serves a purpose. Some deities rule over natural elements. Neptune is the god of water. Vulcan presides over fire. Others oversee human activities. Ceres, the goddess of grain, helps farmers. Mars, the god of war, brings victory to soldiers.

Family relationships were important to Romans. Roman gods and goddesses had families just as humans did. Sometimes a god or goddess would have a child with a human. These half-god children could have

Neptune is sometimes depicted riding a chariot pulled by horses from the sea.

VULCAN'S ANGER

Vulcan is the Roman god of fire. The word *volcano* is derived from his name. When Mount Vesuvius, in what is now Italy, erupted in 79 CE, Romans thought Vulcan was angry with them. The city of Pompeii was destroyed by the eruption. For hundreds of years, it lay hidden beneath a layer of ash and soil. Archaeologists discovered the remains of the city in 1748. Today, Pompeii is one of the most famous archaeological sites in Italy.

special powers. They form an important link between the Romans and their gods.

MAJOR ROMAN GODS

Janus is the god of beginnings and endings. Romans believed he could see the future. He is usually shown with two faces, one looking to the future and the other to the past.

Saturn is the god of agriculture. Saturn taught the people of Rome how to grow crops. He is often shown with a scythe, a tool with a curved blade used for cutting crops, in his hand. His festival, Saturnalia,

Romans sometimes showed Jupiter holding thunderbolts.

took place around the time of the winter solstice
in December.

Romans worshipped Jupiter as the ruler of the sky
and the king of the gods. Jupiter is deeply involved in
human affairs. Romans always sought his approval and
support. Jupiter's symbol is the eagle. His wife, Juno, is
the goddess of marriage.

Mars is the Roman god of war. Rome was a military society. Mars was one of its most important gods. Mars defended Rome against its enemies and aided the army in its conquests. On his festival day, March 1, his priests carried replicas of his sacred shield around the city.

THE GREEK CONNECTION

The Romans admired the ancient Greeks. They adapted many Greek gods, goddesses, and myths to their own culture. For this reason, Roman deities may be very similar, or even identical, to Greek deities, just with different names. Sometimes, the name did not even change. For instance, both Greeks and Romans worshipped Apollo, the god of the sun, music, art, and poetry.

Pluto is the god of the underworld. He is the source of metals mined from the earth. He also rules caves, underground rivers, and the dead. He is often shown with keys. These keys unlock the gates to the underworld. Once a

Roman gods and goddesses, including Minerva, have been popular subjects of art for centuries.

dead soul passes through the gates, it can never return to the land of the living.

MAJOR ROMAN GODDESSES

Juno, the wife of Jupiter, is the goddess of marriage. She serves as the protector of the married women of Rome. Juno and Jupiter do not always get along, but together they form a strong couple. Juno's symbol is the Milky Way.

Minerva is the goddess of wisdom. Her symbol is the owl. Minerva rules over writing and medicine. As an expert weaver, she also protects craftspeople. Together with Diana and Vesta, she is one of three unmarried goddesses who are devoted to their work. At times, she was also associated with war. Romans held a festival to celebrate Minerva from the 19th to the 23rd of March.

Diana is the goddess of the hunt and also of the moon. Romans saw her as a strong, independent woman. She aids hunters and was one of the most widely worshipped goddesses in Rome. One of her largest temples stood on the Aventine Hill. According to some historians, men were not allowed to enter.

Vesta is the goddess of the home, especially of the hearth, or fireplace. Romans considered the hearth to be the heart of the house. Vesta was one of Rome's most beloved goddesses. Her priestesses kept a fire burning in her temple to protect the city of Rome from harm.

EXPLORE ONLINE

Chapter Two introduces gods and goddesses of Roman mythology. Visit the website below to learn about the everyday lives of ancient Romans, as well as the role mythology played in Roman life. Does the information on the website answer any questions you had about Roman mythology?

BBC: WHAT WAS LIFE LIKE IN ANCIENT ROME?

abdocorelibrary.com/roman-mythology

CHAPTER THREE

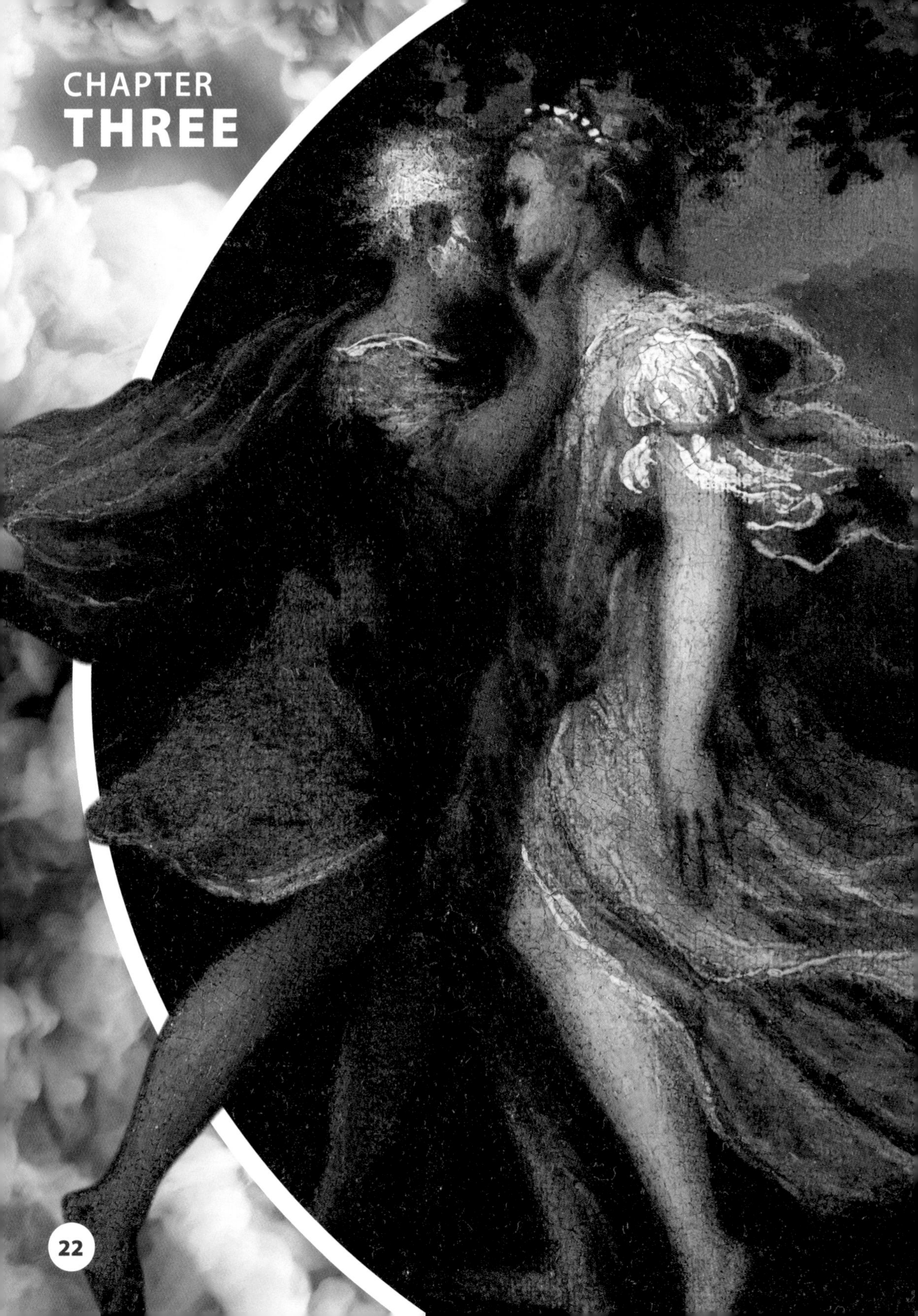

LEGENDARY CREATURES

In Roman mythology, humans can take on animal forms. Animals, too, can often act, speak, and feel as humans do. Romans were very interested in natural history. Some of their legendary creatures were similar to those found in nature. Others combined human and animal characteristics. In Roman mythology, legendary creatures are often deadly to humans, but some can also be friendly.

FRIGHTENING CREATURES

Roman legends tell of the basilisk, a snake that can kill just by looking at someone. Sometimes it is described as half snake and half bird. It has brilliant feathers and a crest like a rooster.

Sometimes gods fall in love with nymphs.

Basilisks appear in Greek mythology, too. According to one story, a basilisk can die of fear by seeing its own reflection in a mirror.

A catoblepas is another frightening creature: it resembles a bull with an enormous head. Like the basilisk, it can kill with its gaze. Because its head is so heavy, however, it spends most of its time looking down. The Roman writer Pliny the Elder describes the catoblepas as living in Africa, where it eats poisonous bushes and trees.

PLINY'S NATURAL HISTORY

Born in 23 CE, Pliny the Elder was a Roman soldier and writer. His 37-volume book _Natural History_ describes thousands of animals, plants, minerals, and geographical formations. Pliny did not always base his descriptions on his own observations. He included many stories he heard from others. Pliny died in 79 CE while trying to save people from the volcanic eruption at Pompeii, Italy.

BASILISCO· (sive regulus grevini)

BASILISCO (in solitudine Affricæ)

The basilisk is sometimes shown with legs and other times without legs.

GOATS, HORSES, AND WOLVES

Fauns are playful creatures, half-human and half-goat. They were named for the god Faunus, who rules the forests. Fauns live in the forest. They play flutes and other musical instruments. Though mischievous, they are not considered dangerous. Nymphs live in the forest, too, and are often seen with fauns. Nymphs are spirits that look like beautiful young girls. Like fauns, they love to sing and dance.

CANIS THE FAMILIAR

Canis lupus familiaris may sound like a legendary creature, but it's really the scientific name for dogs. Wherever Romans went, they took their language, Latin, with them. Latin became known as the common tongue because so many people from different groups spoke it. Scientists still use Latin to describe and classify plants and animals. Dogs descend from gray wolves, whose scientific name is *Canis lupus*. *Canis* means dog, *lupus* means wolf, and *familiaris* means familiar or domesticated (bred to live with humans).

The Ethiopian Pegasus is a winged horse like the Greek Pegasus, but with horns like an antelope. It lives in Ethiopia. Some stories say it can roar like a lion. It is not afraid of people and will stand its ground if confronted in the wild.

Wolves are very important in Roman mythology. Fierce and loyal to their families, they display the traits Romans valued. According to one story, men could turn into wolves by swimming across a particular lake. After nine years, they could swim back and become men again, as long as they had not attacked any humans while in wolf form. The Romans called these unfortunate creatures *lycanthropus,* which is Latin for "wolf-man." Today, people call them werewolves.

FURTHER EVIDENCE

Chapter Three discusses creatures in Roman mythology. What is the main point of this chapter? Find two or three pieces of evidence that support the main point of this chapter. Then visit the website below. Find a quote that relates to this chapter's main point. What new information or evidence does it add?

PBS: THE ROMAN EMPIRE IN THE FIRST CENTURY: MYTHOLOGY

abdocorelibrary.com/roman-mythology

CHAPTER FOUR

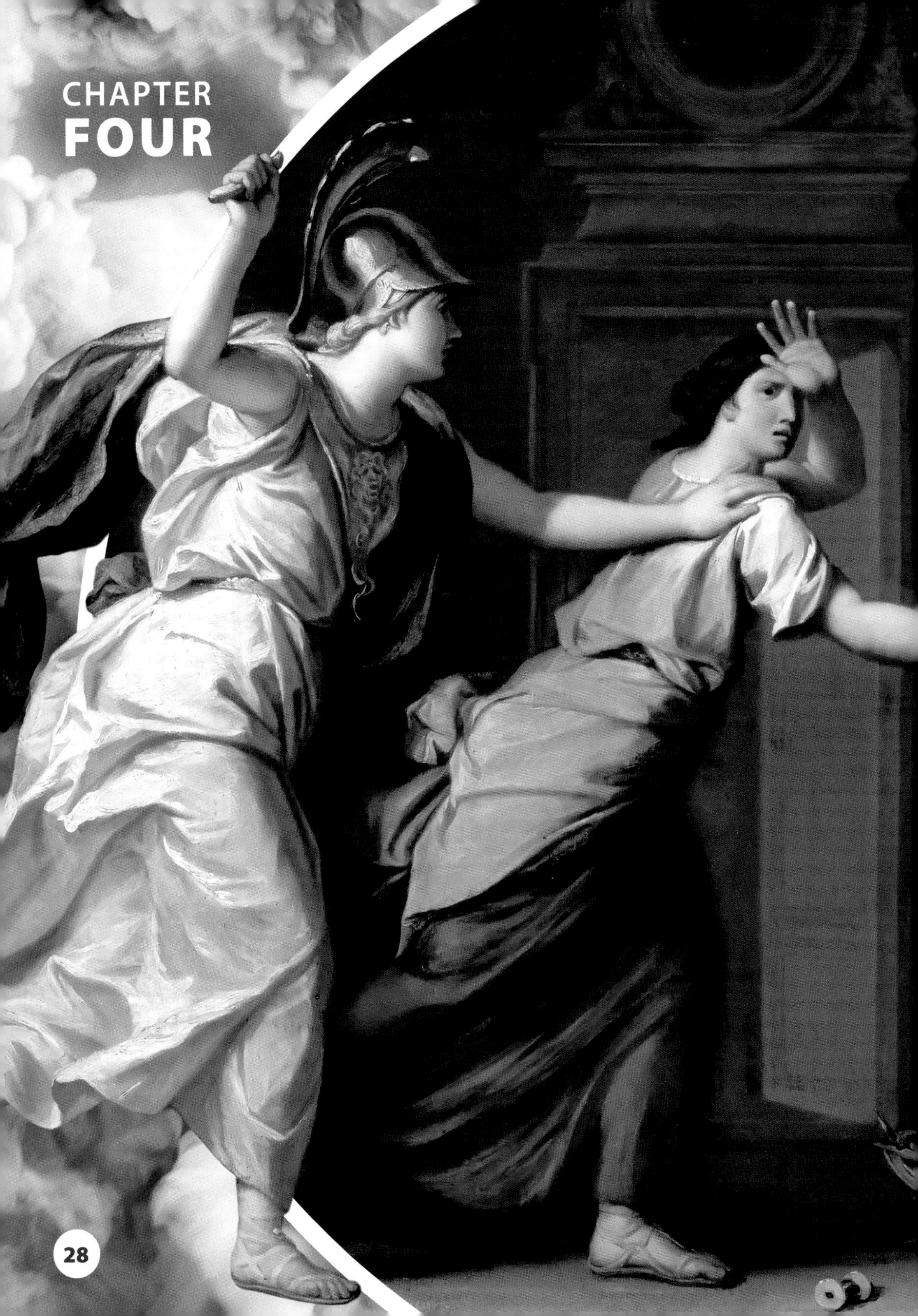

STORIES FROM ROMAN MYTHOLOGY

Roman myths have many purposes. Some explain historical or natural events. Others explain the origins of animals or plants. The myths are intense and filled with action. They often involve interactions between humans and supernatural beings, including gods and half-gods. In Roman mythology, gods and goddesses have emotions and desires just as humans do. Their stories involve love, rivalry, fear, and courage. Every human feeling is revealed at

Out of jealousy, Minerva, *left*, turned Arachne into a spider.

one time or another in Roman myths.

MINERVA AND ARACHNE

The goddess Minerva was an expert weaver. One day she overheard the human girl Arachne bragging that she was a better weaver than Minerva. Minerva became jealous. She disguised herself as an old woman and challenged Arachne to a contest. Each wove a tapestry showing different Roman myths in brilliant colors. After seeing the tapestries, Minerva knew that Arachne was a better weaver, but still wanted to punish her for bragging. She changed Arachne into a spider so she would spend the rest of her life weaving. The name

Diana often wears a crescent moon crown in artwork.

arachne, which is Greek for "spider," formed the word
arachnid in English.

DIANA AND APOLLO

In addition to ruling over hunters, Diana was the
goddess of the moon. Her brother Apollo was the god

of the sun. He draws the sun across the sky with his chariot. One day, Apollo's son drove the chariot instead. The sun ended up scorching Earth. Diana watched in horror as people and animals suffered. After Apollo's son left, darkness fell. Diana, as the moon, sent water in the form of dew to heal the earth. Romans believed the moon was linked to water and that it had special healing powers.

AENEAS THE HERO

The Trojan soldier Aeneas was one of Rome's greatest heroes. After he fought the Greeks in the Trojan War, he traveled with his fellow Trojans to Italy. Aeneas wanted to live in peace, but Turnus, the leader of the Rutulians, saw him as an invader. Turnus tried to drive the Trojans away. The god Jupiter favored Aeneas. Jupiter's wife, the goddess Juno, favored Turnus. The two men fought several battles. Jupiter and Juno argued until Jupiter convinced Juno that Aeneas was the better warrior.

Aeneas had to flee Troy when the Greeks won. He carried his elderly father out of the city.

VIRGIL'S *AENEID*

The Roman poet Virgil wrote an epic poem (a long story with many adventures) about Aeneas called the *Aeneid*. Born in 70 BCE, Virgil studied Greek poets when he was young. When he grew up, he traveled to Greece, where he learned about Greek history and culture. The *Aeneid* tells the story of how Aeneas came to Rome and settled there. The poem mixes many Greek and Roman myths. Today, the *Aeneid* is considered one of the great works of world literature.

Juno abandoned Turnus. Aeneas won. He and his Trojans settled in Italy. Aeneas brought Greek culture and learning to Italy. Romulus and Remus were said to be the descendants of Aeneas. Because of this, Romans considered Aeneas to be the father of their nation.

STRAIGHT TO THE
SOURCE

In this selection from the *Aeneid*, Virgil uses images from nature to describe Aeneas and his enemy Turnus in their final battle (laurels are a kind of tree):

> The way the two, Aeneas and Turnus, were,
>
> Was as, in a forest, two fires, come in from both sides,
>
> And blaze with a seething noise in the laurels, or as,
>
> From a mountaintop come down, two rivers wildly
>
> Roaring, and as they reach the level ground
>
> Bring everything in their way that there is, to ruin.
>
> These two, Aeneas and Turnus, rush into battle,
>
> Their hearts are bursting with fury. . . .

Source: Virgil. *The Aeneid*. Translated by David Ferry. Chicago: University of Chicago, 2017. Print. 397.

What's the Big Idea?
Read the passage over carefully. What is the main idea in this passage? What words and images does the author use to convey that idea?

MAGRIPPALFCOSTERTIVMFECI

ROMAN MYTHOLOGY IN TODAY'S WORLD

The Roman Empire was vast. It stretched over Europe and parts of Asia and Africa. The influence of Roman culture, ideas, and language spread too. Many English words are based on Roman mythology. The word *cereal* comes from the name of Ceres, the Roman goddess of grain. The word *martial,* as in *martial arts*, describes things related to war and combat. It comes from the name of Mars, the Roman god of war.

People can still see many Roman temples today.

Sculptures of Janus still stand in Italy.

Some months of the year also take their names from figures and events in Roman mythology. January got its name from Janus, the god of beginnings. February is named for Februa, an ancient Roman festival held during that time of year. March was the month of Mars. June was the month of Juno, the goddess of marriage.

Throughout Western history, writers and artists have been inspired by Roman deities, legendary creatures, and stories. For example, the basilisk appears in *Harry Potter and the Chamber of Secrets* by J. K. Rowling.

GODS IN THE SKY

One way to see Roman gods and goddesses in today's world is to look up. Ancient Romans studied the sky for signs and omens. They believed many of their gods and goddesses lived in the sky. They named five of the brightest objects in the night sky after their gods. Though they

APOLLO LANDS ON THE MOON

Both the Romans and the Greeks worshipped the god Apollo. In the 1960s, NASA created the Apollo space program. The goal was to land on the moon. On July 20, 1969, two US astronauts landed on the moon in a spacecraft called the lunar module. They left the spacecraft and took the first ever walk on the moon.

didn't know it, these objects were planets. As new planets were discovered, astronomers kept the tradition and named them after Roman gods. Except for Earth, all the planets in our solar system, including the dwarf planet Pluto, are named after Greek or Roman gods. Three of the largest known asteroids are named after the Roman goddesses Ceres, Vesta, and Juno. Today, these names for planetary objects are used throughout the world, demonstrating the wide influence of Roman mythology.

SOLAR
SYSTEM

Seven of the eight planets are named after Roman gods. One, Uranus, is named after a Greek god. Pluto is a dwarf planet. Why do you think astronomers continued naming planets after Roman gods?

Sun

Mercury
God of Travel

Venus
Goddess of Beauty

Earth

Mars
God of War

Jupiter
King of the Gods

Saturn
God of Agriculture

Uranus God of the Sky
(Greek, Roman equivalent is Caelus)

Neptune God of Water

Pluto
God of the Underworld
(dwarf planet)

FAST FACTS

Gods and Goddesses

- Diana is the goddess of the hunt.

- Janus is the god of beginnings and endings.

- Juno is the goddess of marriage.

- Jupiter is the king of the gods.

- Mars is the god of war.

- Minerva is the goddess of wisdom and sometimes war.

- Pluto is the god of the underworld.

- Saturn is the god of agriculture.

- Vesta is the goddess of the home.

Creatures

- The basilisk is a deadly reptile.

- The catoblepas is a monstrous creature resembling a bull.

- Fauns are mischievous creatures that are half goat, half man.

- The Ethiopian Pegasus is a winged horse with horns found in Africa.

- A lycanthropus, or werewolf, is a human who has changed into a wolf.

Stories

- Romulus and Remus were twin brothers nursed by a wolf. They founded Rome.

- The tale of Minerva and Arachne tells how the goddess Minerva became jealous when a girl named Arachne boasted about her weaving skills. To punish the girl, Minerva turned Arachne into a spider.

- A story of Diana and Apollo tells how Diana, ruler of the Moon, healed the earth with dew after Apollo's son scorched it with Apollo's chariot.

- Romans told of how Aeneas of Troy came to Italy and conquered his enemy Turnus. Aeneas is the ancestor of Romulus and Remus.

STOP AND
THINK

Surprise Me

Chapter Three discusses legendary creatures of Roman mythology. After reading this book, what two or three facts about legendary creatures of Roman mythology did you find most surprising? Write a few sentences about each fact. Why did you find each fact surprising?

Tell the Tale

Chapter Four retells several stories from Roman mythology. Choose one story and, without looking back at it, rewrite the story as if you were telling it to a friend. Try to remember as many details as you can. Add your own details to make it interesting. What stayed the same from the story in the book? What is different?

Dig Deeper

After reading this book, what questions do you still have about Roman mythology? With an adult's help, find a few reliable sources that can help you answer your questions. Write a paragraph about what you learned.

Say What?

Studying Roman mythology can mean learning a lot of new vocabulary. Find five words in this book you've never heard before. Use a dictionary to find out what they mean. Then write the meanings in your own words, and use each word in a new sentence.

GLOSSARY

aqueduct
a system of pipes and raised canals used to supply water to cities in ancient Rome

asteroid
a small rocky object that orbits the sun

classical
having to do with the culture of ancient Greece and Rome

deity
a god or goddess

empire
a nation that rules over many different territories and people

exile
the state of being banished, or sent away from one's homeland as a punishment

frieze
a mural that goes around the wall of a room or around a building

generation
a group of people born around the same time

oracle
one who can read omens and predict the future

symbol
something that represents something else

temple
a building dedicated to the worship of a god or goddess

ONLINE RESOURCES

To learn more about Roman gods, heroes, and mythology, visit our free resource websites below.

Visit **abdocorelibrary.com** for free Common Core resources for teachers and students, including vetted activities, multimedia, and booklinks, for deeper subject comprehension.

Visit **abdobooklinks.com** for free additional online weblinks for further learning. These links are routinely monitored and updated to provide the most current information available.

LEARN MORE

James, Simon. *Ancient Rome*. Relaunch ed. New York: DK, 2015.

Williams, Marcia. *The Romans*. Somerville, MA: Candlewick Press, 2013.

INDEX

About the Author

Patrice Sherman is the author of many books for young readers. She has written on topics ranging from colonial America to the history of magic. Her favorite Roman goddess is Minerva, the goddess of learning and wisdom.